Emily Harrison combines precise writing and bold performance, both of which are underpinned by an unflinching honesty. A former member of The Barbican Young Poets, Emily performs regularly in London and across the UK both as a member of The Burn After Reading Collective and a solo performer. In 2010, Emily won Oxford University's Christopher Tower Poetry Prize. She has been published in *Popshot*, *Rising* and was one of eight poets to have their work on the theme of London showcased at Boxpark, Shoreditch.

EMILY HARRISON

I CAN'T SLEEP 'CAUSE MY BED'S ON FIRE

Burning Eye

This edition published by Burning Eye Books 2016

www.burningeye.co.uk
@burningeyebooks

Burning Eye Books
15 West Hill, Portishead, BS20 6LG

ISBN 978-1-909-136-71-7

I CAN'T SLEEP 'CAUSE MY BED'S ON FIRE

CONTENTS

For Josh

STOCKHOLM SYNDROME

The perfect love story,
the kind where opposites attract.
Problem is he works for the NHS
and I'm detained under the Mental Health Act.

Sure, it's not easy to trust someone's emotions
when they've just met you
but just because I've only been in love forty-five minutes
doesn't make it any less true,
and just because all my rights have basically been taken off me
doesn't mean we can't make it through.
I don't want just anybody to escort me on my half-hour leave;
I just want you.

Sure, they can assign you another case
and you'll have other patients every once in a while
but I know it's you checking my file,
thinking, *Oh, wow, she's so interesting,*
look at how much interesting shit
they've mistaken for a mental disorder.
And I know you know too it's out of order
they think they can keep us apart
with six-inch-thick bulletproof glass.
Well, let them.
Let them dismiss it.
But next time I'm sedated
for getting manic during *Countdown*
just kiss me and risk it.

And, sure, you might only be free
to see me at medication time
but all couples have problems
and all couples find the time,
schedule permitting,
to talk about the day, their dreams,
how they read the complete history
of agricultural developments in Nigeria in one sitting.
And they talk about the weather.
I just think we'd be great together.

Ten years' time, we'll be sat down at dinner and we'll laugh
about how they used to write in my notes
I should be restrained by 'only female members of staff'.
And I'll be adamant that I knew you loved me
in every single way
when you simply asked
during a routine blood test,
'Emily, how are you doing today?'

QUINOA IS ONLY SPELT LIKE THAT TO OUT THE WORKING CLASS

The junior doctor
doesn't need to prove anything to the dinner table.

He says it all when boasting,
                  'I now have the power to section people.'

I see the child
pretending
to drop the priceless vase
with over-dramatic unstable hands.

The rich kid showing off his remote-controlled
                        whatever it is.

The big red 'press me but you really shouldn't press me'
button.

He's one of those
filling up my wine glass without my permission,
drowning my food in gravy
when I specifically said
    just a little bit.

Someone actually laughs.

And I sit in my highchair
all oblivious smiles with food face,
the only one who had to ask for a napkin

The fork in the right hand, the knife in the wrong hand,
stop hitting yourself.

At least if someone chokes on their food
or, God forbid, their words
we're in safe hands

I force in another profiterole.
Revenge is a dish served best to whoever prepped it.

UFOS IN THE MASK OF TUTANKHAMUN

I walk into the room.

Before I can say anything
a man with butcher's fingers
points me back out.

'This is addiction,' he says.

I stare longingly
at the back
of a fan oven.

I do not think that man
is very good at his job.

£6.31

I want you to show me
an appropriate occasion to wear stilettos
where the room assumes you are sleeping with me
simply because you allowed me in it.

I want you to take me
to the kind of restaurants where you order bread for the table
and by British stoicism alone
you will force my chair
to shift from one leg to the other.

You are the kind of boy
I would be too embarrassed
to make a homemade gift for.

I can imagine your fantasies:
me spit-polishing your boots,
yelling how much I make an hour
whilst you spank me with a rolled-up map of your family tree.

And I will know my place and take it,
sinking my NHS teeth into your venison and
spilling cheap Chardonnay on those corduroys.

You are the kind of boy
I would lie to
about everything.

INTRAVENOUS CUISINE

It's okay
because we've got the wind-turbine view
and the parking doesn't run out
for another two hours.

It's okay to sit like it might not be,
to treat it as a dinner party
where one guest is in bed at the table
all cutlery and drip.

We're politely ignoring the backless robe and
the hand sanitiser between courses,
noticing, 'You didn't eat much,
are you feeling okay?'

That warm disinfected piss smell
scraping your tonsils
is to remind you you've never been cleaner;
that the safest places are more machine than people.

And it's all okay
because tomorrow their lights will wake me
and despite it being June
they will make me think it's Christmas.

BEREAVED MISTRESS SHOWING UP TO THE FUNERAL AGAINST THE FAMILY'S WISHES

The heels sinking into the soil,
his favourites.
The dress,
the one she saw
on his credit card bill.

Hair pinned back
to expose shoulders.
Lipstick shade: tantrum.
I rejected the fishnets.
What more do they want?

Kneel at the graveside
to show off the perfect curve.
Exaggerate weeping
the way we practised.
Fake guilt
like fistfuls of mud.

If we are to sin,
we must sin quietly.

I think of him
removing strands of hair
from the passenger seat,
sending letters to me
from a different post box
each time.

As they lower him,
she cries.
But we both know I am the favourite.

Her holding the Bible,
me with dirty knees.

SWINDON MAKES ME FEEL LIKE A RUSSIAN BRIDE

Boxes ticked then stamped
with excessive saliva
with recycled customs
recycled red white and blue

Arrive all catalogue smile and foldaway legs
laughing and nodding and laughing
dragged to football games by barcode wrists
refuse public affection
reject catering van hotdog
envy real trophy lifted by real man

Continue applying lipstick as absolute necessity
continue laughing and nodding
and laughing and weeping
in the toilets of a country pub

Learn churned-out marriage manual
that taught you Sputnik highs
Tchaikovsky crescendos on dress rehearsal bananas
and to always remember to say thank you
afterwards

All Power to the Imagination!

Lie back
and think of Novosibirsk

MILAD'S GIRLFRIEND

Cross-legged in front of the wardrobe mirror
she puts on the face
along with the second-date dress she chose
for memories' sake.
Her fingernails match the toenail polish he won't see
but it makes her feel better.
She always wears the heels.

We hear her coming
all the way from the gynaecology ward.
No one in here knows her name.
Milad stands by the ping-pong table,
the awkward prom proposal without the flowers.

A staff member has to let her in
and we know to leave them a meeting room.
They laugh and they talk and they kiss
about anything other than this.
Visiting hours go on longer when she's here.

Before he leaves he perches her on the edge
of the ping-pong table
as seven psychiatric patients look on.
A staff member yells, 'That's it, end of visiting hours.'
She whispers into his neck,
a staff member yells that visiting hours are over.

She holds his face in her hands
and with the sternness of a cattle prod says,
'Do not cheat on me in here.'
A staff member yells
and she is escorted out.

Milad stands by the door until he can't hear her anymore.
No one knows her name,
she just always wears the heels.

OIL ON CANVAS

There is always a phone
and a box of tissues
as if they might one day encourage me
to enact a conversation with God,
a modern-day confessional.

I'm heaving defence tactics that would give
Broadmoor walls a run for their money.

If she were so nice
then the sign in the toilet saying
        Now Wash Your Hands
would have included a *Please*
and she wouldn't
tarmac over today's problem
by asking about so long ago.

I forget the words to the serenity prayer
trying to explain the anxiety of a family meal.

I look in her folder when she leaves to take a call
expecting grotesquely-drawn caricatures of idiotic patients,
mocking speech bubbles full of ridiculous misdirected things
        she tapeworms out of them
but it's just a scribbling reminder of Deb's birthday.

When she returns
her short sleeves are mocking me

And when she doesn't let me use the stapler
because 'it might be triggering'
the large flesh-coloured canvas in reception
with red paint kung-fued up the length of it
really starts taking the piss.

My homework is to learn serenity
by rote rather than by feeling
and I remember the words that evening
when the waitress switches me to steak knife.

BAKE OFF

I knew you weren't the one
when you wouldn't let me
lick the bowl clean.
The 'you' in 'you shouldn't eat raw eggs'
not a caring sentiment reserved for me
but obviously something you'd read online,
typed by the single digit
of a Dettol-wielding
middle-class mother
terrified of eggs and cow's milk,
the common cold
and a little bit of harmless food poisoning.

NO, I DO NOT OWN A CAT

It's the third day of sun in a row but
I forget what warmth feels like on bare skin.

I cut thumb holes in my school jumper
to hold the sleeves down.

I dream
of tarmacking over my arms.

At college
I buy a sharpener every week,
couple it with a Christmas-cracker screwdriver.

Everyone becomes an evangelist:
all children can be healed but
at eighteen you're on your own.

I spend days
imagining pitchfork parents
calling me a bad influence.

And I practise the same response to myself:
'No, I do not own a cat.'

THE JUKEBOX CRIES OUT FOR ITS MOTHER

Something as small

as an ear bone shifts
and the result
        is tectonic

First you lose
contact with an old friend
        and time sits disappointed

You promised
        you'd keep
                in touch

Sleep throttles you
in a fit of jealousy

Afternoon resuscitates

Toothpaste dribble
Avoid reflection
        like plague

Alphabetise everything

Deserted spoon
sits disappointed

Knife and fork
talk behind
your back

Time won't return
your phone calls

Leave answerphone message

Sit until legs
go blue

Cry hollow
        Start again

I'D LIKE TO THANK THE ACADEMY
(TIPS ON GETTING PROZAC FROM YOUR GP)

If you spend all night online researching
you'll convince yourself you can blag it.

It's like taking a practical exam
with the instruction manual left open beside you,
taking an eye test with your contacts left in,
being handed a script
of the most incredibly inspirational, against-all-odds biopic
about the harrowing life of a disadvantaged genius
(who also happens to be extremely attractive)
and being asked to play the lead part.

I'd like to thank the Academy.

When they ask where your mood is on the scale
tell them you're a 6 out of 10
never a 5 out of 10
and if you were a 4, you'd be speaking more slowly –

maybe speak more slowly

but not too slow
else you might appear to be at a 3
and that's when the questionnaires come out.

I'd like to thank everyone who made this possible.

Say you're hopeful for the future,
you understand things will take time to stabilise
but that ultimately you're feeling a little more yourself.
Do not mention that you think you are Jesus Christ.

I'd like to thank God.

Remember eye contact,
enough to look engaged;
maybe nod every now and again

but don't overdo it. Don't stare.
No nodding and staring and nodding and staring.
That's when the injections come out.

I'd like to thank the director.

The hardest part will be keeping your leg still.
It's making the whole desk shake.
Well, move back.
Regret the lipstick and the short skirt
and try not to eye flirt.
For God's sake do not eye flirt.
Put your eyes away.
You can see the wedding ring
(I'd like to thank my father).
That photo frame probably has pictures of his kids in.
Stop staring, stop nodding, keep that leg still,
and do not, do not lick your lips
Come on, we're better than this.

Never look at the prescription pad.
Your whole mouth will fill with saliva,
you'll swallow loads
and everyone knows guilty people gulp loud.
Change the subject.
'So, I see you're married…'

And slowly the world sees how untalented you really are.

Acting as bad as feigning shock
when you won the damn thing.

I'd like to thank all the other nominees.

Leave the appointment at this point.
Go home and rehearse.

Because before you know it you're the actor
that needs to think of their mother's funeral
when the love of their life leaves them
just to get a tear.
You're accidentally acknowledging the camera.
Behind-the-scenes footage is leaked
of you yelling at the lighting guy,
possibly throwing a coffee in his direction
but that's for the courts to decide.

Do not become the ageing actress
yelling bitterly about the new leading lady,
waving a cigarette in one hand
and holding the Oscar in the other.

I'd like to thank the Academy.

SMART/CASUAL

Dressed up all Cluedo for Kinks,
Miss Scarlet Latex
in the dungeon
with the double-ended dildo.

He'd taken too many pills,
I'd overdosed on make-up.
A trip to A&E was inevitable.

A waiting room full of
Thursday evening accidents
watched me prop him up
in the plastic seat
then equally struggle to sit in mine,
squeaking like a wet rubber marigold.
No Madonna or whore question about it,
they skipped straight to asking,
'Do you think she'll charge him extra for this?'

They got to keep their secrets,
each one of them
the naked pervert in the stained anorak
straddling park puddles
revelling in the reflection.

ENERGY WASTED ON STANDBY

For years I've bled
and kicked and flipped and thrashed.
I've done jazz hands
until I got whiplash.
I've regurgitated
deep-seated emotional issues
to aid my artistic development
and, on demand, I've smiled.
My psychiatrist said
I got into theatre
because I wasn't hugged enough
as a child.

All my life
I've overstudied
to be an understudy.

Less like a shadow,
more like dandruff
or toenail clippings,
scabs on shins and kneecaps,
or sweat on the pillow,
saliva on fingertips on banknotes,
piss on public toilet taps.

Last week I hit a relapse.

Wednesday afternoon
I see her waiting
at the crossing in town.
Green man says Walk,
car radio says Mow Her Down.
My foot over the accelerator
makes the skin between my toes itch;
I ignore my psychiatrist's instructions
to let it pass
and listen to my left eye twitch.

I ask myself if I can be trusted
not to waste time
reversing back over her
when I really need the head start.
And what if she doesn't break
that slender neck?
(The one that got her the fucking part.)
I think, I can be more creative than this,
more careful not to leave a mark or bruise.
I'll choke her with her rave reviews,
convince the whole world and myself
it was an act of grandiose egotism
when she's found
with the *Great London Theatre Guide*
protruding out of her mouth.

HIGH AND DRY

I was picked up
in an off-licence
as an afterthought.

She's not the kind of girl
to ever check the weather.

'Pay under a fiver
and don't be surprised
if it's a singer-server.'

She makes me want to shrink down
so I can fit in her piña colada

but she'll only let me out
in drizzle.

The upmarket one for when it's pouring
lingerie lace
curvaceous dome
a handle that'll hook you in.

She's the kind of girl
that won't let a bit of precipitation
stop her flirtation.

This won't be her first time under transparent PVC.

You can see her
all eyes and thighs
at the same time

and men collapse in on themselves,

birds,
broken wings mid-flight,
in a constant state of falling.

TELL ME I ASKED FOR IT

For Lolita

I refused to buy the copy
with the young girl's
photograph on the cover.
I had seen those eyes before
smiling two-thirds full
only because someone else had drunk the rest without asking.

My first copy was bought as a gift
by a man with therapist's knuckles
and no PhD
who thought 'underage' was just a bourgeoisie term,
that if your muse is too old
then you're faking it.

I read my own copy on the tube
behind heart-shaped sunglasses,
vetting men
and their curious looks,
owing her
everything.

Writing a novel is not punishment enough,

Humbert, your heart is rotten
and your poetry fucking sucks.

BETWEEN TWO PEOPLE

I tried to be charmingly awkward
       another typewriter types
       about how I tuck my hair behind my ear and giggle
       and how my eyes are swimmable

I tried to be inappropriately hilarious
       a painting falls off the wall
       and bounces off the coffin

I tried to be undeniably sexy
       a tennis player's thighs grunt
       short skirt sweats
       in a dozen-telly window display

I ended up a single serviette
handed over cautiously by the waitress
between two people
       one crying at the thought of dying alone
         the other having no idea why

NAN'S COCONUT CAKES

We used to ring the bell
on the way down the stairs
to let everyone know you'd been to the toilet.

We'd take Granddad's alcoholic miniatures
and play doctors and nurses.

Her fridge had a magnet
from every county in England
and a tea towel to match.

I asked her once why she had such a colourful carpet and
she said, 'With so many grandchildren
you need something to hide the stains.'

If you ask me
I can tell you exactly what builds a home:
more photographs than your mind's got memories,
two hundred and thirty-six cherry brandy miniatures,
matching armchairs
and a mortgage.

FOR DISPLAY PURPOSES ONLY

Jacqui leaves old orange peel and banana skin on my radiator,
says it smells just like potpourri.
To me it's week-old bin liner on a hot day
but I don't have the heart to tell her that.

When a nurse asks,
I don't want to drop Jacqui in it.
I adopt her backward thinking reluctantly,
explain word for word
until the word *potpourri* loses all meaning.
He nods himself through it like I did.
It's not that he doesn't have the heart to tell me,
he doesn't have the time.
There isn't a box for that on the form
and he's only allowed one Biro.

The last time I dobbed Jacqui in
they took her artwork away.
She got 7.5mg and couldn't talk without dribbling.

From my window
I can see across the courtyard
into the maximum security ward.
I watch violent outbursts.
I watch forced sedation.
I watch men of my father's generation
lose every way of expressing themselves
because talking therapy never suited them.
And now they sit in armchairs –
        the 'if you're sat on it you can't throw it' theory.
They watch paint climb the walls –
        the 'stare at it long enough and it disappears' therapy.
They wait for nothing to happen
twice.

Over this side we know when to let things slide.
I'm staring hard at everything, hoping it all just disappears.

Everything,
except the smell of burning orange peel
and the word *potpourri*.

I CAN'T SLEEP 'CAUSE MY BED'S ON FIRE

I turn to a nurse and say,
'If there's one place you can't be embarrassed about your
dance moves,
it's in a psych ward.'
I had joked earlier, sat down plastic next to Danny.
'What you get?'
'Double vodka Coke.'
We find courage
thumbing the ridges of the vending machine cup.

Tonight, Friday night, is a game of musical paper plates.
It's much harder to drag someone up to the dance floor
without physical contact
but slowly others join us
as if someone held up a huge cardboard sign
telling them they were allowed to.
Danny, arm in sling, does his best to show off and to me
it looks like the first time he has ever danced.

I watch from the fence,
his pupils sink,
as if with a hard enough wish
he could turn water into wine.

I LOOK ON ALL THE WORLD AS MY PARISH

I didn't understand
why we were colouring in
John the Baptist again
with the same
sharpened-down colouring pencils
that no longer fit the tray they live in.

They replace last year's picture
with this year's picture.
We've just stayed within the lines this time.

Sunday school took place
in the hall beneath the church.
Off-limits stage and ballet bars without the mirrors.
Self-reflection was never encouraged

and neither was sneaking around the garden.
No one was buried in this one.
I remember it was there
that I first saw a millipede.

They taught us Satan invented the question mark
and when told Jesus died for my sins
I honestly thought he shouldn't have bothered.

Shrove Tuesday 1999,
me and Jonathan make pancakes.
Flipping from one side to the other,
he asked as inoffensively as palm crosses,
'You don't actually believe all this, do you?'

I thought when the moment came
it would bite like lemon
but this juice came from a plastic bottle.
I shrugged and asked him to pass the sugar.

Still, to this day,
that was the sweetest pancake I have ever tasted.

VIEW OF A SEAGULL

The dead seagull
didn't look peaceful
or sleeping;
it just looked dead.

Rejected by its own species,
seagulls mock
as they swoop in.

I walk home
the next day
specifically
to see it gone,
wondering what got at it first:
the foxes
or the amateur taxidermists?

COUNT TO ZEN

He thrusts at me
all the cologne-sting charm of
Richard Gere:
unshaven unshowered unshackled,
high on sleazy sour sex
with his flies undone.

Twelve-point plans
precise as voodoo needles,
speeches so impressive
he'd chew off his own tongue
sure he'd never better it.

I mourn the recently deceased
British stiff upper lip,
force family hugs on strangers.
One woman waterfalls tears
from my rigor mortis shoulders
down my back.

Confused by unhygienic embraces,
mouth full of someone else's cardigan fibres,
the world's most arrogant man
acting as the wind
to my Marilyn skirt
drags me by my ankles
into enlightenment.

Lolling heads gawp at him
stuck on the victim carousel.
He salivates green and grins money,
splitting stitches
as he rough-hands his wallet
and stuffs suffer money like
last week's newspaper.

Nausea sticks itself
to the roof of my mouth
and I am the only one to notice

what enlightenment really means
when I see the picture of his
wallet window wife
on a cruise.

And she smiles like a pin-up
on the side of a 1940s bomber.

A LITTLE BIT NUTTY AND A LITTLE BIT SLUTTY

She made the mistake
of dismissing what a wedding ring meant
because she didn't have one herself.

Falling in love
with the kind of men
who encourage dangerous behaviour
whilst telling you
that with those scars you can't be a ballet dancer.

Now Monica can't wear blue
without the ladies from the church congregation
whispering over shopping carts,
holding husbands' arms tight,
marking territory the way they label homemade jam.

And we all told Monica
that the fault lies
in silly little girls who act grown up
when they aren't grown up at all.

Because you're the kind of fun
that runs parallel to wives and responsibility;
to the company account
as opposed to joint savings.

You're the Friday evening that never touches the Sunday
lunchtime.

The phone call always hidden by the hand
that gets condensation on the mouthpiece.

FOUR-MATCH BAN

Vinnie Jones is acting badly on the telly
slamming someone's head
in a car door
over and over
when you shoulder-barge in with
'I know how to hit you and not leave a mark'

I dream of giving you
the fastest red card in history

Vinnie keeps slamming
and thoughts splinter
Vinnie keeps slamming
reducing memories to dust

The room clenches its teeth

Vinnie Jones is acting badly on the telly
and your intentions are
blunt hooligans' fists
your intentions are
claret on a sovereign ring

I never thought I'd learn
that covering your face isn't instinct
and that violence
is only ever slow motion
on screen

THE GIRL WITH THE JADE EARRINGS

Your Edvard Munch rip-offs,
seven feet tall,
loomed like bad decisions.
Fairground mirrors
laughed at both of us.

You were living on a blow-up mattress.

Stacks of Prozac
in the corner of the room
where the books should have been,
stolen to be sold as
plastic surgery for the soul.

I regretted boasting to your friends
that I might be on the telly.

I flinched like a brush stroke
until you'd had enough of waiting.
Your eyes pinned me down and said,
'Let's give The Scream a reason
to pull a face like that.'

The bed deflated,
became a see-saw
where we'd never find common ground.
You pulled everything down to my ankles,
dragged me along the carpet.

An elbow to the face
I still want to believe was an accident.

I focused all of my energy
on finding a pair of jade earrings
I'd taken off for safekeeping,
a gift from Kaya.
I wasn't leaving her here again.

And when you chased me out into the street
complaining you didn't have my number,
it was raining.
Of course it was raining.
It needed to.

SLALOM

Jacqui smokes in the quad,
resurrecting old boyfriends.
A ski instructor broke her heart once
with LSD and diamonds.
She talks about the relationship
alongside downhill skiing.
It cuts like wind
on top of the Alps.

FOUR-POSTER

Never beg a stranger for empathy
same ward
same bed
different situation

I spit a grit smile
at the girl opposite
she just does not
smile back
guilt hits tear ducts
nostrils
molars
especially when her mum
gives an unapologetic entrance
common but not in courtesy
screams 'not this shit again'
iron clasp on painful wrists
drags her daughter
as butcher dragging chump steak
drags her daughter
as I dragged dolls with one shoe
as I dragged you

and my mum
tired
from sleeping in an upright chair all night
gives me that look
that was four years coming

SEVEN WAYS OF LOOKING AT A CROW

1. I don't care where yours came from.
He was born
        from a shoebox
                in a tent
                in Savernake Forest.

2. Done counting rhinestone-snatcher second-bests,
                        one is my lucky number.

3. The only book I have ever asked to be spanked with.

4.   I wanted you to get the gun.
                        I wanted you to empty the tree.
                        I was trying to make a Chekhov play out of us.

5. Carry you on my back, Ted.
        Heavy as kitchen appliances
and not always as useful.

6. I got drunk at a party and told Edgar Allan Poe to fuck off.

7. Guests say it's the eyes that creep them out the most.
Those aren't even his eyes
        but what could be hurting so much.

TOY SOLDIERS

Jumping off the stage
you'd just read a poem
about your granddad
that made me cry.

I picture the photograph
your mother showed me.
That brass-buttoned cardigan,
the one she had so much trouble
convincing her stubborn toddler to wear.

I wish I'd known you forever.

You smile at me
with those pretty big blues
and wipe a bogey on the underside of the table.

SONNET FOR ROBERT

It's the first day of big school
and
you tell me your huge orange Puffa jacket is to stop you
getting cold
rather than to keep you warm.

We balance dominoes in the eye of the storm.
You cry because everyone is an unfriendly giant
and I don't because I'm a responsible adult now.

We are Hansel and Gretel:
fairy-tale terrified.

On the way to the dining hall
you leave a trail of fingernails bitten to bleeding bone.

We both wince at the ice-cream scoop
used to serve mashed potato,
sit and count peas like minutes to the end of the lesson.

Whenever the bell rings it rips the teddy bear from your hands
and replaces it with a textbook labelled *Tough Love*
that doesn't have any pictures in it
and you panic.

To ease the stress
we fill up whoopee cushion lungs
pretending to blow out birthday candles
and when air reaches maximum capacity
you still look over to me with self-doubt.

You're half my age, Robert,
but you seem to be blowing twice as many out.

T-CUT

He smiles like he needs only two front teeth and barely speaks.
I spend my childhood talking for him,
inherited his rod-straight spine and the ability to never let
sympathy
leak into empathy.

We sat in the car the first time,
his white Mondeo R reg., he said that sometimes
the headaches are so painful it's like a frontal lobe
chainsaw.

That summer insomnia cut off his middle finger with the
lawnmower.

One day he gets out of the shower and complains
about the wet-dog smell
and the postman
won't come to the front door.

We are told to watch out for cling-film eyes,
a crimson ring around the bathtub,
and if he starts Bible quotes
we know the number to ring.

He dances like his shins are being bitten.

Three years later I am home for the summer.
An accident at the factory
leaves him scarred.

We have a bonding session.

We say things that sound like they could be said to anybody
but when I mention those bastard headaches
his stare sets like when credits roll
without him noticing.

He's cleaned the same spot on the car fifteen times already.
I'm waiting for the colour to rub off.

FIVE-STAR FISH BAR

I've never bought chips there
but the man behind the counter
waves at me
in our unspoken routine
each time I walk past.

XXL sky-blue T-shirt,
the way you'd think of God's as big,
patterned with batter and fat.

He wipes his greasy hands in ritual
for a holy Sunday wave.

I have never bought chips there,
never known how many of those stars
he really deserves,

but his smile,
vinegar-soaked and wide as London,
gets Friday thumbs up,
Tuesday top marks.

Some days he is lost
to the *Sporting Life*
and jars of pickled eggs
and some days his huge back is turned
serving saveloy instead of smiles.

The days I miss him
my train is always late.

TO STRANGERS WHO GIVE LIFE ADVICE
WITHOUT REALISING IT

I told him over breakfast
I share the bed
with an overactive imagination.
A haunted B&B
was not my first choice.
His laugh startled me,
shook the fried egg.

He spoke of Wenlock cinema, 1973,
opening night of *The Exorcist*.
Everyone made paper aeroplanes
out of the warning information.
They set them free
at first sight of the possessed girl,
a flock of distraction.

Hitchcock would have been proud.

It was the first time his had flown,
no accidental boomerang.
This time his laugh was reassuring.
Poltergeists are better for business.
He winked,
took the sheet off the ghost
and laid it on the table.

GO HOME AND STOP GRINNING AT EVERYONE

You all want something from me:
attention to warm your eyelashes,
face-down laughter,
molars grinding into carpets,
a bullied pelvis,
a broken jaw,
the last Rolo.

ACKNOWLEDGEMENTS

Thanks to my friends and family for their relentless love.
An old-fashioned thank you to Tim Wells.
This book would not be here without the NHS.

Poems included in the collection have been published in the *Morning Star*, *Rising*, *Stand Up and Spit*, and *Street Sounds*.

Lightning Source UK Ltd.
Milton Keynes UK
UKOW02f1426170416

272350UK00002B/28/P